The White Card

ALSO BY CLAUDIA RANKINE

Poetry

Citizen: An American Lyric
Don't Let Me Be Lonely: An American Lyric
Plot
The End of the Alphabet
Nothing in Nature Is Private

Play

The Provenance of Beauty: A South Bronx Travelogue

Coeditor

The Racial Imaginary
American Poets in the 21st Century
American Women Poets in the 21st Century

The White Card

A Play in One Act

CLAUDIA RANKINE

Graywolf Press

This publication is made possible, in part, by the voters of Minnesota through a Minnesota State Arts Board Operating Support grant, thanks to a legislative appropriation from the arts and cultural heritage fund, and a grant from the Wells Fargo Foundation. Significant support has also been provided by Target, the McKnight Foundation, the Lannan Foundation, the Amazon Literary Partnership, and other generous contributions from foundations, corporations, and individuals. To these organizations and individuals we offer our heartfelt thanks.

Published by Graywolf Press
250 Third Avenue North, Suite 600
Minneapolis, Minnesota 55401

www.graywolfpress.org

Published in the United States of America

ISBN 978-1-55597-839-6

2 4 6 8 9 7 5 3 1
First Graywolf Printing, 2019

Library of Congress Control Number: 2018947087

Cover design: John Lucas

Cover art: Martha Tuttle

The White Card opened on February 28, 2018, in collaboration with ArtsEmerson and the American Repertory Theater, at the Emerson Paramount Center on the Robert J. Orchard Stage in Boston, Massachusetts, with the following cast:

CHARLOTTE CUMMINGS	*Karen Pittman*
CHARLES HAMILTON SPENCER	*Daniel Gerroll*
VIRGINIA COMPTON SPENCER	*Patricia Kalember*
ERIC SCHMIDT	*Jim Poulos*
ALEX COMPTON-SPENCER	*Colton Ryan*

Director: Diane Paulus
Dramaturgy: P. Carl
Scenic Design: Riccardo Hernandez
Costume Design: Emilio Sosa
Lighting Design: Stephen Strawbridge
Sound Design: Will Pickens
Projection Design: Peter Nigrini
Associate Director: Carl Cofield
Production Stage Manager: Sharika Niles
Casting: Stephen Kopel, CSA

PREFACE

One evening during a question-and-answer session, a white, middle-aged man stood up. After movingly addressing my reading from *Citizen*, he asked me, "What can I do for you? How can I help you?" As I stood on stage regarding him, I wondered how to move his question away from me, my story, my body to the more relevant issues and dynamics regarding American history and white guilt. Teju Cole's essay "The White-Savior Industrial Complex" came back to me in that moment. Maybe it would have been better to use Cole's words directly, to quote his extension of Hannah Arendt into the realm of whiteness: "The banality of evil transmutes into the banality of sentimentality. The world is nothing but a problem to be solved by enthusiasm." Or this: "The White Savior Industrial Complex is not about justice. It is about having a big emotional experience that validates privilege."

But in the moment, I decided to climb out from behind all my reading, references, and quotes and engage his question *personally* without the distancing scaffold of referential-speak. His question struck me as an age-old defensive shield against identifying with acts of racism at the hands of liberal, well-meaning white people, the kind he had just listened to me read. His question did the almost-imperceptible work of positioning him outside the problems *Citizen* interrogates, while maintaining his position of superiority relative to me in his act of offering to help me. He would help answer not only my problems but those of all black people, which he only at that moment recognized but otherwise was not implicated in or touched by. He seemed oblivious to the realization that our problems as a society are dependent on his presence, despite my project of saying this in all the ways I know how.

The afterlife of white supremacy (to appropriate and flip on its head Saidiya Hartman's "the afterlife of slavery") is all our problem. Cole writes, "All he sees is need, and he sees no need to reason out the need for the need." If he were to reason out the need for the need, he would understand he need not invite himself to the scene. He is already there. There was so much that could be said about the often-meaningless reparative largesse of whiteness in the face of human pain and suffering, but in the minutes we had for our exchange, I simply responded to the man, "I think the question you should be asking is what *you* can do for *you*."

He didn't appreciate my answer.

From inside his theater of noblesse oblige, which seems to come close to condescension but really exists in the depths of repression of American complicity with structural antiblack racism, rose an anger that I confess I didn't expect. "If that is how you answer questions," he responded, "then no one will ask you anything."

The germinal thought, the originating impulse, of *The White Card* came out of this man's question and his response to my response. In his imagination, Where did I go wrong? Was I initially intended to express gratitude for his interest? Were his feelings and the feelings of the audience in general my first priority? Was recognition of his likability a necessary gateway into his ability to apprehend my work? I really wanted to have the conversation he started. I didn't come all this way not to engage but as the affect theorist Lauren Berlant has stated, "What does it do to one's attachment to life to have constantly to navigate atmospheres of white humorlessness."

It occurred to me after this incident that an audience member might read all the relevant books on racism, see all the documentaries and films, and know the "correct" phrases to mention, but in the moment of dialogue or confrontation retreat into a space of defensiveness, anger, silence, which is to say he might retreat into the comfort of control, which begins by putting me back in my imagined place. Perhaps any discussion of racism does not begin from a position of equality for those involved. Maybe the expectation is for the performance of something I as a black woman cannot see even as I object to its presence. Perhaps the only way to explore this known and yet invisible dynamic is to get in a room and act it out.

Theater is by its very nature a space for and of encounter. The writing of *The White Card* was a way to test an imagined conversation regarding race and racism among strangers. The dinner party as a social setting for the sharing of both space and conversation in the home of a white family seemed the benevolent, natural, if not exactly neutral, site. The characters have come together to consider the terms of an exchange of art, while they get to know one another. What brings everyone to the room is a desire to be seen and known, but what keeps them there is the complexity of our human desire to be understood.

This play could not have been written without the conversation and support of Catherine Barnett, Lauren Berlant, Allison Coudert, Diane Paulus, and P. Carl. Thank you to David Dower and David Howse for commissioning the work, Diane Borger and Ryan Michael Sweeney for developing the work, and to ArtsEmerson and American Repertory Theater for directing and producing *The White Card*.

CLAUDIA RANKINE

The White Card

CHARACTERS

CHARLOTTE CUMMINGS: *female, black.* Yale MFA graduate, forty-ish. Her most recent collection of work uses photography. She has received major prizes and is on the verge of breaking into the international art market. Her mother is a lawyer for the ACLU and her father is an epidemiologist at Columbia-Presbyterian Hospital and a professor at Columbia University.

ERIC SCHMIDT: *male, white.* Dealer, early forties. The great-grandson of Anton Franz Schmidt, who founded one of the most prestigious art galleries in New York. Eric is a connoisseur of modern conceptual art and a strong advocate of young progressive artists. He has been instrumental in shaping the Spencer Art Collection for the last decade and is on the board of the Spencer Art Foundation.

CHARLES HAMILTON SPENCER: *male, white.* Entrepreneur, art collector, early sixties. Highly knowledgeable, well connected to political figures and businessmen, he is a lover of contemporary art who made his money in real estate. He is also a well-respected philanthropist who is interested in ideas around diversity.

VIRGINIA COMPTON SPENCER: *female, white.* Charles's wife, fifty-five to sixty. She is interested in art and in her late twenties was an art consultant for corporate clients. They have been married thirty years and have two sons.

ALEX COMPTON-SPENCER: *male, white.* Twenty, a junior at Columbia University, and an activist. Deeply involved in current American politics, he is passionate as he sees the injustices in America. He sees his parents as part of the problem.

Scene One

IMAGE ON REVERSE

Glenn Ligon, *Hands*
(monumental silkscreen of news photograph
from the 1995 Million Man March)

The sounds of a tennis match. The living/dining room is a tastefully elegant and spare NYC loft. In the room is contemporary work by artists representing the victimization of African Americans and Rauschenberg's White Painting. They are well lit and prominent in the space. The art pieces are projected on canvasses around the white room. Everything in the room is white except for the art. The round dining table gestures toward dinner but need not have actual settings. Over the mantel is a piece of art covered by a cloth. At the back of the stage, doors lead onto a terrace. If possible the audience surrounds the dinner party to enable audience members to also be looking at each other.

This is a lovely Saturday night in Tribeca, March 2017. The new administration has been in office for three months and the Spencers are awaiting their guest. From the balcony the city lights are in full view. Eric, Charles, and Virginia are watching the Australian Open a month after it aired.

VIRGINIA: Serena is a beauty.

ERIC: I prefer Venus.

VIRGINIA: They're both stunning.

ERIC: You're stunning.

VIRGINIA: Well, I suppose all people are stunning—what's your issue with Serena?

ERIC: I don't have to love everyone. In any case, she's okay.

CHARLES: Okay? Serena is anything but.

VIRGINIA: Who would have thought the sisters would play
             each other again in a final this late in their ca-
             reers. My favorite thing is watching Serena win.

ERIC: Why are you watching if you know the outcome?
             What fun is that?

VIRGINIA: I don't watch her until after; I get too nervous.
             But I did want to see the Australian Open finals
             before the next Grand Slam came around. Can
             you tell she's pregnant?

CHARLES: (*looking at TV*) She's pregnant? While she's
             competing?

ERIC: I read she got some hormonal rush from the preg-
             nancy. People were complaining it was an unfair
             advantage.

VIRGINIA: Now, that's insane. I spent my first trimesters be-
             tween the bathroom and the sofa. Why are men
             so challenged by the Williams sisters?

ERIC: I don't have a problem—

CHARLES: (*interrupting*) She means men like that Russian
             tennis guy from a few years ago? That was the
             worst.

VIRGINIA: He said they were scary to look at.

CHARLES: I vaguely remember him calling the sisters "brothers" or something like that.

VIRGINIA: It's no different from what was said about the former first lady.

CHARLES: That I distinctly remember.

VIRGINIA: It's hard to forget.

ERIC: Remind me.

VIRGINIA: An ape in high heels.

ERIC: Some guy actually said that?

VIRGINIA: A woman in government.

ERIC: A woman? Wow. People. Jesus. Charles, I thought we might just check in before Charlotte arrives.

CHARLES: What's on your mind? (*Charles hands Eric an hors d'oeuvre and a napkin.*)

ERIC: Where's Lily?

CHARLES: We've given Lily the night off. Virginia thought the evening would be more informal that way.

ERIC: Ah, I understand.

VIRGINIA: Anything we should know?

ERIC: No, no, no. She's lovely. Charlotte's one of us. I
                    just wanted to touch base regarding a few things.

CHARLES: Yes, of course.

ERIC: Remember, she hasn't committed to giving us the
                    new series and she's not doing individual pieces.

VIRGINIA: That must take other collectors out of the
                    running.

ERIC: Almost everyone, all the way out. She knows
                    that to be collected by you will send her prices
                    up here in New York but also in London,
                    Zurich, and L.A. In the past, she has refused
                    some collectors on principle, but I know that
                    won't be a problem here.

VIRGINIA: What do you mean refuse?

ERIC: Some artists can't separate themselves from their
                    work. I think she's one of those. She doesn't have
                    children; the work is everything to her—so she
                    won't sell it to just anybody. She needs the col-
                    lector to be invested in the spirit of the work. She
                    needs money, yeah, but it can be tricky with her.

CHARLES: That makes sense to me. I imagine we'll be her
                    perfect collaborators.

VIRGINIA: Does she know Charles is interested in the pieces
                    we saw in Miami?

CHARLES: Eric says those are committed. Will she bring a
               sample of the new work?

ERIC: I billed this as just a dinner. I hope that's okay.
               She's not showing the new work to anyone at this
               point, but from what she's told me, it sounds very
               compelling.

CHARLES: But still with an emphasis on racial injustice?

ERIC: Still elegiac.

(*Doorbell rings.*)

VIRGINIA: That must be her now.

(*No one moves.*)

ERIC: Is someone going to let her in?

VIRGINIA: Oh right. Charles?

ERIC: I'll let her in. (*He goes to get the door.*)

CHARLES: And where is Alex?

VIRGINIA: I told him to be here by seven.

CHARLES: As if he does anything we tell him.

VIRGINIA: Go easy tonight.

(Eric reenters with Charlotte.)

ERIC: Virginia, Charles—It's my pleasure to present the artist of the twenty-first century.

CHARLES: My dear Ms. Cummings. So good of you to come.

CHARLOTTE: Please call me Charlotte.

CHARLES: Your picture doesn't do you justice. We saw your impressive work at Art Basel and the Armory. And of course the photo-collages from Ferguson are unforgettable.

VIRGINIA: I'm Virginia. Welcome.

CHARLOTTE: Thank you.

VIRGINIA: Your coat? Charles, do take Charlotte's coat. Eric says we haven't met, but I know we've been introduced. We met at Jack Shainman Gallery.

CHARLOTTE: I don't . . .

ERIC: Jack Shainman? I introduced you to . . . that wasn't Charlotte.

VIRGINIA: Yes it was.

CHARLES: I assume it's champagne all around.

CHARLOTTE:	Thank you. You have a beautiful home. Wow, you have one of Rauschenberg's White Paintings. The light on it makes everything really . . . bright.
CHARLES:	Despite the fact they are monochromatic it's amazing how much it changes with the light. It was curated to brighten the room.
VIRGINIA:	Actually, it's just a piece I wanted. Charles curated the rest. It's a lot of history to see every day. Luckily most of them are at the foundation.
ERIC:	These here are some of the works that are most meaningful to Charles.
CHARLES:	Not all the artists are African American, but all the work considers the violence against them.
ERIC:	Charlotte's work is what's missing from our collection.
VIRGINIA:	Charles likes to wear his commitment on the walls. I personally can think of other places for him to put it, but we agree to disagree. Don't we, sweetheart?
CHARLES:	I guess we do. Charlotte, do you know Robert Longo's work? This one is untitled but it's of Ferguson police, August 13, 2014. His work critiques fascism.
CHARLOTTE:	Hmmm, I'm not sure I understand how fascism's being critiqued.

CHARLES: All that white, smoky charcoal obscuring the faceless police? I—

VIRGINIA: (*interrupting*) I like it. It's atmospheric and not as graphic.

CHARLOTTE: That's my point.

ERIC: If I remember correctly the painting is based on an actual photograph.

CHARLES: You know it is.

VIRGINIA: Eric likes to pretend he doesn't know all he knows. Isn't that right, Eric?

CHARLOTTE: (*playful*) He's the epitome of humility.

CHARLES: He knows good work when he sees it. And so do I.

ERIC: Charlotte, I think that's meant for you.

VIRGINIA: Yes, Charlotte, all eyes are on you.

CHARLOTTE: My friends say such good things about working with you. Glenn Ligon was so pleased we were finally connecting.

CHARLES: Glenn, yes. We have a number of his pieces, but this one here is from the Million Man March. It's an early piece focusing on the social and economic stresses that black men face.

VIRGINIA: Come, let me show you this other piece. It's called *Defacement: The Death of Michael . . . Michael Stewart*, that's right. He was a Pratt student, graffiti artist, who was beaten into a coma by police. He died. This is about as real as I can handle it.

CHARLOTTE: I've never seen this Basquiat. It takes my breath away.

VIRGINIA: We just acquired it. It's all Charles looks at.

CHARLOTTE: There's so much to see. I've read about your collection in *Artforum*. So many artists here who have inspired me. I'm really honored to be with you tonight.

VIRGINIA: We're delighted that you're here as well. Charles takes his stable of artists quite seriously. For him you're not just an investment, he believes you're leading a conversation with the culture.

(*Charlotte and Virginia move away to look at the Basquiat. Eric sees a piece covered by a cloth. He turns to Charles.*)

ERIC: Charles, are you acquiring art behind my back?

CHARLES: Oh, no, no, this is something special! Someone brought it directly to me.

ERIC: Should I be worried?

CHARLES: You? Never. I'm surprised you'd even ask that. You're practically a member of this family.

ERIC: Can we see it?

CHARLES: After Alex arrives. We acquired it with him in mind.

ERIC: You didn't mention Alex would be joining us.

CHARLES: He should be here any minute. We thought he'd enjoy meeting Charlotte.

ERIC: I wish I'd known he was coming. The last time . . .

(*Virginia and Charlotte approach.*)

CHARLES: No worries, man. His interests and Charlotte's work align. *They* will be on the same page. Ginny wants to do an unveiling of the new piece after dinner. You know how much she loves curating our experiences. (*Turning to Charlotte.*) Our son Alex will be joining us. Despite the fact that the election is history now, I'm delighted to say he's at a Trump rally.

CHARLOTTE: You don't mean he supports . . .

VIRGINIA: Oh, no, quite the opposite. Charles meant to say protest, not rally.

CHARLES: (*laughs*) My dear, don't worry, you're safe here. Since the election Alex is even more politically

engaged than he was before. I hardly know
when he has time for classes. Every day there's
another rally.

VIRGINIA/ERIC: Protest.

CHARLOTTE: Charles isn't wrong. The president throws himself
rallies. He threw one in Florida.

CHARLES: College students were extremely invested in this
election.

VIRGINIA: In Bernie . . . I'm not sure that they voted.

CHARLOTTE: He must have been crushed. Is he your only child?

VIRGINIA: Is he our only child, Charles?

CHARLES: (*shooting Virginia a look*) Alex has an older
brother. And make no mistake, we were all
crushed.

ERIC: (*cutting in*) Virginia, you are looking fabulous as
always. Still playing tennis?

VIRGINIA: Pilates. These past weeks the closest I get to
a court is thinking about Serena. (*Turns to
Charlotte.*) We were just TiVoing the Australian
Open when you arrived.

CHARLES: Ginny doesn't do real time! Bad for the stress lines.

VIRGINIA: Steady. (*To Charlotte.*) Do you play?

CHARLOTTE: Yes, I do. At the Greenvale Club.

VIRGINIA: That's where I play, too, but it's getting too diffi-
                cult to get a court. Too many people there now.

CHARLES: What should I be worried about when we play?

CHARLOTTE: Not much. I wish I could serve like Serena.

CHARLES: Not so long ago she was unbeatable.

CHARLOTTE: Did you know she's pregnant?

VIRGINIA: Yes, we were just discussing that. She's really ma-
                tured. A couple of years ago she went back to
                Indian Wells despite what happened there . . .
                Charles, you remember, we were there, the usual
                racial slurs . . . the sisters boycotted it for years.
                (*Turning to Charlotte.*) Isn't that right?

CHARLOTTE: Objecting to racism means you're childish?

ERIC: Similar things were said about Colin Kaepernick.

CHARLES: I'm not sure about his method. Kneeling during
                the national anthem is unnecessarily provocative.
                But he's right about the injustice. Anyone for
                more champagne?

ERIC: I won't twist your arm. Charlotte, we're so ex-
                cited about your new work. Why don't you tell
                us what you're doing?

CHARLOTTE: Well, I like to think of myself as a bit of an archaeologist. I've always been interested in what gets lost . . . who gets left out of the picture.

VIRGINIA: Lost?

CHARLOTTE: Made invisible. The writer Teju Cole says, "We need to think with our eyes."

VIRGINIA: I'm still reading the book by that other fabulous black author . . . Ta Ta . . .

ERIC: Ta-Neheezi Coates.

CHARLOTTE: Ta-Nehisi . . .

ERIC: Isn't that what I said?

VIRGINIA: That's it . . . Ta-Nehisi. *The World between Us.* I'm sure you've read it.

CHARLOTTE: Yes, *Between the World and Me.* I love when Coates says he wants his son to know that no matter what happens he always has people.

CHARLES: Speaking of people, I enjoyed the piece he wrote called "My Obama."

CHARLOTTE: I loved that. "My Black President" I think it was called.

VIRGINIA: You're both wrong. The piece is called "My President Was Black."

CHARLES: Charlotte, dear, what were you saying about Teju
              Cole's work?

CHARLOTTE: Only that I'm intrigued by *his* interest in how we
              think about the unseen . . . how we make what's
              unseen visible. I guess you could say Coates is
              doing the same thing.

VIRGINIA: Is that the ambition you have for yourself? I mean,
              for your work?

CHARLOTTE: Ambition? I do want people to experience what
              black people are feeling, or if that's unreasonable,
              at the very least, to recognize what it means to
              live precariously.

VIRGINIA: (*genuine feeling*) What kinds of feelings am I not
              feeling?

CHARLES: That's why your work is so important to people
              like us.

CHARLOTTE: Inasmuch as the work makes visible things that
              white people might not have to negotiate in the
              day-to-day, it might seem that way . . .

VIRGINIA: But what kinds of feelings?

CHARLOTTE: Mourning for dead strangers with whom I share
              only one thing.

VIRGINIA: I feel terrible for all those mothers who lost
              their sons.

CHARLES: And daughters, Ginny. I think Charlotte means race as the shared attribute.

CHARLOTTE: I did. But the work doesn't exist from a single perspective. All those dead men, women, and children have mothers and fathers. It's true.

ERIC: Her creative process involves staging her pictures.

CHARLOTTE: I'm trying to bring into focus events that are immediately forgotten. I realized the only way to capture passing moments was to restage and photograph. You know Jeff Wall's approach?

ERIC: I've always been interested in Wall's decision to reenact moments that he's missed. His photographs portray what he calls existing "unfreedoms."

CHARLES: "Unfreedoms"?

ERIC: Reactions that happen before you have time to think—

VIRGINIA: Our son Alex uses the term microaggression. Is that the same thing?

CHARLOTTE: I don't know exactly what Wall was thinking. Clutching your purse or crossing the street when a black man approaches comes to mind as something people do.

ERIC: Still, he rarely deals with race.

CHARLOTTE:	Racism, you mean. There's his *Invisible Man* piece.
ERIC:	I can only think of his image *Mimic*, where a guy points to his eyes as he walks by an Asian man. I'd say your current work differs in significant ways.
CHARLOTTE:	My early work really wasn't procedurally that different, to be honest.
ERIC:	That's true. Charlotte started by staging small inadvertent aggressions that are overlooked or repressed in our day-to-day life.
CHARLOTTE:	For example, once I was in the subway and I watched a middle-aged white guy so intent on where he was going he didn't see he'd knocked over my cousin's daughter. We were all heading back from a tennis match at Flushing Meadows actually.
ERIC:	She restaged it and was able to catch the moment the child hit the ground.
VIRGINIA:	You had someone knock down a child so you could take a picture?
CHARLOTTE:	Yes, I mean, no. The child was an actor.
VIRGINIA:	So, yes.
ERIC:	She's fine. She practiced falling.

CHARLOTTE: But that's not what . . . my point is it's difficult to see the violence, the ownership of public space, all of that.

VIRGINIA: So, the reenactments depend on your interpretation of the moment. But how much are you creating the moment rather than reflecting it?

CHARLES: That's what all great art grapples with.

CHARLOTTE: Any moment can be made ordinary, but when you're in the moment you know precisely what's happening.

VIRGINIA: Just the other day a beautiful woman held the door open for me and a line of white men just flooded through. I wondered why she didn't just let it slam in their faces. You could have definitely taken a picture of that, Charlotte.

CHARLOTTE: By beautiful do you mean black?

VIRGINIA: She was black but she was beautiful.

(*Alex enters the room.*)

VIRGINIA: Alex!

CHARLES: You're finally here.

ALEX: This was as soon as I could get here.

CHARLES: We want to hear about the rally . . .

VIRGINIA/CHARLOTTE/ERIC/ALEX: Protest.

CHARLES: Protest, but let's start you off with a glass of
                  champagne.

VIRGINIA: You know Eric. This is our new friend Charlotte.
                  (*Alex walks over to Charlotte and hugs her to her
                  surprise.*) Sweetie, so what happened today? How
                  are your Black Lives Matter friends holding up?

ERIC: (*jokingly*) Isn't that a terrorist group?

ALEX: Don't joke, last year there was actually a peti-
                  tion circling to have BLM classified as terrorists.
                  This administration has decided to focus on what
                  they're calling "black-identity extremists" instead
                  of white homegrown terrorists.

CHARLOTTE: Do you think the protests are helping?

ALEX :   I don't ask myself that question. I show up.
                  This afternoon we gathered on Madison to pro-
                  test the Muslim ban. More white women than
                  usual, probably because of the Women's March.
                  Everything was pretty chill. The police were
                  sympathetic.

ERIC: Thanks to Alex we're constantly made aware
                  of the injustices affecting the lives of people of
                  color, immigrants, Arabs, Palestinians, the
                  undocumented, the queer community, especially
                  trans people, the incarcerated . . . Did I forget
                  anyone?

VIRGINIA:	Alex is really making us think about our own privilege. It's not that I didn't think about it before, of course, but . . . well, I really didn't think about it before! (*Everyone laughs except Alex.*) You know even Charles didn't think about it, and he has spent his life fighting for other people's civil rights.
CHARLES:	Alex reminds us daily that everything matters, including the art we collect. This is the reason we're especially glad you're here, Charlotte. We realize the cultural impact that your art can have.
ERIC:	Hear, hear! But what makes Charlotte's art great is its excellence. Exquisite craft, married to a profound knowing—
CHARLOTTE:	(*interrupts*) You should always talk about my work after a few glasses of champagne.
CHARLES:	Eric is dead serious. We want artists whose work engages the issues at their very core. Engagement must be central to their artistic practice. They can't be distracted.
VIRGINIA:	Why don't you let Charlotte have dinner before you launch into your foundation speeches.
CHARLES:	Ginny's commitment does not supersede the dinner bell.
VIRGINIA:	That's right. I'm committed to the people I see in front of me first.

CHARLOTTE:	Alex, how long have you been involved with BLM?
ALEX:	Well, I signed up after I heard Alicia Garza speak about Trayvon Martin's murder. I'm also a member of SURJ. You must know it.
CHARLOTTE:	No, I hadn't heard of it. I'm no activist.
ALEX:	BLM, SURJ . . . we're all co-organizing around what's going on.
VIRGINIA:	You haven't mentioned SURJ to me.
ALEX:	SURJ, Showing Up for Racial Justice, is for organizing white people. Many want to mobilize but don't know what to do. We mean to move seven million whites—that's three point five percent of the population—forward on racial justice issues.
ERIC:	How's that working out for you?
CHARLOTTE:	That's an impressive goal, Alex.
VIRGINIA:	Honestly, I feel Alex is a superhero.
ALEX:	Mom, I try to engage with you nonjudgmentally, but you're making it impossible. This isn't about me. We've talked about this before.
VIRGINIA:	Don't lean against the artwork, dear.
CHARLES:	Eric says the new work is even more powerful and complex. What can you tell us about it?

CHARLOTTE:	I'm staging the aftermath of the Charleston crime shootings. I'm thinking more about how art can provoke connection and recognition by reenacting moments of violence that are lost to history entirely.
ERIC:	She's staging the actual crime scene.
VIRGINIA:	Crime scene?
CHARLOTTE:	Yes, that crime scene has never been seen, unlike all of the images from Ferguson that were tragically so public.
VIRGINIA:	Doesn't it depress you? I can't imagine thinking about violence twenty-four/seven.
CHARLES:	(*ignoring Virginia*) How did you get access to the images?
ERIC:	She attended Dylann Roof's trial.
VIRGINIA:	Oh.
ALEX:	Roof's trial was supposed to be in July during the Republican convention, but it was moved until after the election. I found that interesting.
CHARLOTTE:	That *was* interesting.
ERIC:	In any case when Roof murdered nine people in Bible study no images were released to the public.

VIRGINIA: Wasn't that to protect the families? It's not a racial thing.

ALEX: Mom, everything is political. Publishing pictures of Vietnam helped end the war. Why do you think the Bush White House withheld images from Iraq?

VIRGINIA: But *those* were wars.

ALEX: These are wars. Ask Muslims, queers, blacks, immigrants. Did you see the military-grade equipment they hauled out during Ferguson? Come on.

VIRGINIA: There really weren't any public images from Charleston?

CHARLOTTE: Not of the crime scene.

VIRGINIA: I ask Charles this all the time, why would you want to subject an audience to these horrors? I think evidence is important, but why do we need to see endless videos on television, on Facebook, Twitter, Instagram, every place we look . . .

ALEX: Innocent people of color are every place, even if you're trying not to look.

CHARLES: Actually, Virginia, it depends on how you look at it. Think back to the death of Emmett Till in 1955. His own mother wanted the photographs of his open casket to be shown. It energized the civil rights movement.

ALEX:	(*cuts in*) A fourteen-year-old black kid—murdered for whistling at a white woman.
ERIC:	Didn't I just read in the *Times* that the accuser lied about what happened?
ALEX:	No fucking way.
VIRGINIA:	Watch the language.
CHARLOTTE:	Are you surprised?
ERIC:	Old-age confession sort of thing . . . straightening out the accounts before Judgment Day.
CHARLES:	You must think photography could have that same impact now.
CHARLOTTE:	I don't know. It seems like our American pastimes are sports and forgetting. We assimilate; we appropriate; we move on.
VIRGINIA:	But haven't social media changed our general amnesia? I have watched so many killed. I can call up their dying moments on any device in my possession. The phrase "I can't breathe" will never detach itself from Freddie Garner.
ALEX:	Freddie? No, Eric Garner. Freddie Gray and Eric Garner, already they've just become one body for you.

CHARLES: But, Charlotte, you don't see your work influencing the political conversation?

CHARLOTTE: I'm realistic. The work's not on the street, it's in galleries.

ERIC: Like a lot of great art. Think of Goya's *The Disasters of War*, showing the conflict between Napoleon's empire and Spain. Or Turner's *Slave Ship*. Their power is in the execution and mastery, that's what creates the beauty in their works and yours, Charlotte.

CHARLOTTE: Why, thank you.

ALEX: Not if you're black. The work gets reduced to sociology and dismissed as not art.

CHARLOTTE: Well, yes, that's also true. No one talks about how Edward Hopper's nostalgia both reflects and advocates for small-town white America. But he's just seen as a great American artist. No one asks if he wanted to make America great again.

VIRGINIA: I've always liked Hopper. It's curious when people use a contemporary perspective to judge the past. I think emphasizing our differences gets, well, in the way. When Alex joined Black Lives Matter some of the members objected because he was white. Alex went thinking and hoping he could be part of a helpful solution. Isn't that right, sweetheart?

ALEX: I understood why they were suspicious.

VIRGINIA: But why can't all people be helpful? What's our
               purpose then? Are we supposed to do nothing?

CHARLOTTE: What were their objections?

ALEX: Oh, it was nothing.

VIRGINIA: Not nothing . . . a student leader got up and
               said lots of you think you're here helping the
               cause, but what you're doing is just going to
               make you feel better and help you sleep at night.
               Alex said someone even said, they need allies
               not masters. He was judged for just showing up.
               What's wrong with helping and feeling good
               about that?

ALEX: Mom, why do I tell you anything?

VIRGINIA: It infuriated me.

ALEX: It didn't matter.

CHARLOTTE: Sounds to me like someone was expressing anxi-
               ety about white benevolence. I doubt it was about
               Alex specifically.

ALEX: I wasn't the one upset.

VIRGINIA: Well, I would've lost motivation for supporting
               them.

ERIC:	It does seem wrongheaded. How do they expect to get allies if they alienate the very people who have come to help?
CHARLES:	Perhaps anyone who would be alienated by such comments is not a very useful ally. (*Charles and Charlotte eye each other.*)
VIRGINIA:	What?
CHARLOTTE:	The black students were likely responding to a long history of white savior rhetoric.
VIRGINIA:	They have displaced anger if they can't see the difference between those on their side and the real racists.
CHARLOTTE:	The students were angry? Alex?
VIRGINIA:	Don't put words in my mouth. I'm certainly not accusing black people of being angry or unreasonable.
CHARLOTTE:	No?
VIRGINIA:	I'm just saying anger gets us nowhere.
CHARLES:	Darling, shouldn't we check on dinner?
VIRGINIA:	We went to one of Alex's protests. We saw the police pushing him around, I wanted to intervene . . .

ALEX: I was never in danger.

VIRGINIA: What do you mean? You could have been hurt. Do you think Goodman's and Schwerner's mothers were any less worried than Chaney's during the Freedom Summer murders? I know it's not politically correct to say, but to a mother, your life has to matter too.

ALEX: Mom, when you say my life matters in this context you're essentially saying all lives matter. And that's so not the point. Black Lives Matter is about black people actually being human. No one questions the humanity of white people.

VIRGINIA: I understand the point, and still, your life matters.

CHARLOTTE: If I were a mother I don't think that I could have stood there and believed my son wasn't in danger.

VIRGINIA: Exactly.

CHARLOTTE: Not exactly . . .

VIRGINIA: Charles is the one who kept saying don't worry, don't worry . . .

CHARLES: They were on the school grounds. Despite arrests, I knew the administration would have them back in classes by the afternoon, as was the case.

ALEX:	You'll like this, Charlotte. She photographed the police arresting me and she put it on the back of our Christmas card.
CHARLOTTE:	I don't understand.
ALEX:	She sent out this image of me being arrested at that BLM protest as our Christmas card. So wrong on so many levels.
VIRGINIA:	All I wanted to do was show our support for you. I really care about what Alex is doing to make things better.
ALEX:	My work isn't about individual action. It's about working in solidarity against white supremacy. I realize the ways in which my whiteness protects me and that whiteness is tied to the beliefs of white supremacy.
VIRGINIA:	What are you saying? Do you honestly believe *we* are white supremacists?
ALEX:	White privilege is a thing. White people believe they're in charge; they expect shit.
VIRGINIA:	I said watch your language.
CHARLOTTE:	I don't think white people identify themselves as white Americans. They think their perspective is objective. They don't realize they're always invested in the advancement of white people.

VIRGINIA:	How does that differ from white supremacy? You and Alex are going a little too far.
ALEX:	Whenever a black person points out the supremacy of whiteness they are told they're *going too far*.
ERIC:	Excuse me, but you're not black; Virginia was addressing both of you . . . probably you more than Charlotte.
CHARLOTTE:	All we're saying is that whiteness is propped up at every turn. It's its own legacy program. Remember how difficult it was for *Moonlight* to win an Oscar?
CHARLES:	*La La Land.*
ERIC:	That was bizarre. I've been watching the Oscars all my life and I've never seen anything like it. But . . . you think that was some supremacist conspiracy?
CHARLOTTE:	Maybe not, but why did it take that Price Waterhouse guy so long to correct it? White folks don't like to lose.
ERIC:	No one likes to lose.
VIRGINIA:	People make mistakes.
CHARLOTTE:	President Obama had to be sworn in a second time after Justice Roberts mixed up the order of the words.

CHARLES: That hadn't happened before either.

ALEX: It's no wonder black people are angry.

VIRGINIA: Charlotte, I hope you're not angry. These are
            difficult issues. They can't be solved over dinner.
            My god, we haven't fed you? Charlotte, please,
            come this way. We just went informal tonight,
            it's a buffet. Alex, come give me a hand. I got
            your favorite chicken.

*(Virginia exits to the kitchen followed by Charlotte and Alex, leaving
Eric and Charles alone.)*

ERIC: So how do you feel the evening is going?

CHARLES: I like her. I like how measured she is. The new
            work could be really groundbreaking.

ERIC: I agree.

CHARLES: I want to do more than buy her work, I want to
            support her endeavors.

ERIC: She did say something about wanting a new studio.

CHARLES: What do they run nowadays?

ERIC: Depends. Brooklyn. Around a million.

CHARLES: That's not bad. I know someone I can call. I'm
            thinking she'd be good for the board. We have
            that hole there.

ERIC: It will definitely solve the diversity issue.

CHARLES: It will be appropriate to explain the workings of
                     the foundation and the impact it's having.

ERIC: I'll leave that to you. What do you have there?

CHARLES: Oh, I know how discerning you are about wine.
                     Here's something special. This is one of the best
                     pinot noirs I've found.

ERIC: I won't refuse. You know me too well.

(*Charles pours Eric a glass; he sniffs, swirls, and tastes.*)

ERIC: This is a La Tâche, I can tell by its depth and
                     complexity. The darkest red of its kind.

VIRGINIA: (*entering, Charlotte and Alex following*) I see
                     you've tasted Charles's surprise.

ERIC: Yes, it's very elegant.

CHARLES: Ginny, what did I tell you? La Tâche is always a
                     winner.

VIRGINIA: It's a bloodstain, Charlotte. That's how it trans-
                     lates from the French, because of its deep color.

CHARLOTTE: (*she takes a sip*) C'est un des meilleurs millésimes:
                     vous me gâtez vraiment.

VIRGINIA: Everyone, please start.

ERIC: I neglected to tell you Charlotte studied photography in southern France. Arles, was it?

CHARLOTTE: Yes, I attended École nationale supérieure de la photographie.

VIRGINIA: Oh. Lovely, lovely.

(*Everyone eats.*)

CHARLES: Ginny, the chicken's perfect.

ERIC: I love that you've let the fat drip onto the potatoes the way the French do. The only place I've had anything as good is in Avignon. This is heavenly. Fantastic food while being surrounded by such beauty.

ALEX: How can you talk about beauty when we have Nazis in the White House? Didn't you see Sebastian Gorka in his Nazi uniform at the inauguration and the pictures of the Breitbart staff as the Executive Cabinet? In any case they are just an extreme version of the rest of us.

CHARLES: Alex, you have to keep things in perspective. There are also many helpful facts.

ALEX: What helpful facts?

CHARLES: I don't support this idea that all white people are a part of what's wrong in this country. Some of us are working very hard to make all our

	lives better. You can go as far back as President Johnson's role in the Civil Rights Act. There's Obama's presidency. We need to look at the way the system works.
ERIC:	Amen.
CHARLOTTE:	All things can be true at the same time. Like Bryan Stevenson says, the North may have won the war, but the South won the narrative.
ALEX:	See, Dad, you're forgetting some of the facts. The reason you can support Charlotte's work comes in part from the private prisons you construct.
VIRGINIA:	He's got you there, Dad.
(*Silence.*)	
CHARLES:	Everybody knows I'm in real estate and construction and, yes, it's true the state of Ohio contracted with me to build prisons. But prisons are only one of the many things my company builds. We also build hospitals and schools.
ERIC:	Is he any more responsible for what goes on in the prisons than in the hospitals and schools that he builds?
CHARLOTTE:	How do you reconcile yourself to a system that has targeted minorities for profit? How do you make peace with that?

CHARLES: Would it surprise you to know eighty percent of the inmates at the Ohio Reformatory for Women are white.

ALEX: In Ohio maybe . . . of the two point three million people in prison in America, one million are African Americans. That leaves one point three million cells for everyone else. In Maryland alone seventy-two percent of incarcerated prisoners are black. Don't you have a prison there too, Dad?

CHARLES: I am well aware mass incarceration is an important issue for black communities. It might be *the* issue.

CHARLOTTE: You say that, but it really doesn't touch your life.

(*Virginia stands and begins to collect the plates.*)

VIRGINIA: Charles let our son Tim go to prison. He could have used some of those connections of his . . . but he wouldn't. Does that make you feel better, Charlotte?

CHARLES: We're not going over that again and certainly not now.

CHARLOTTE: Feel better?

(*Charlotte stands and tries to help Virginia clear the plates.*)

VIRGINIA: Sit down. You're not the maid. (*Virginia leaves.*)

CHARLES: It seems like someone has had a little too much
               to drink. Charlotte, my apologies.

ERIC: In any case, Charlotte's work addresses . . .

CHARLES: We were speaking about incarceration. I'm not
               going to sugarcoat anything, I have too much re-
               spect for Charlotte. First of all, my company is a
               public company; it answers to its shareholders.

CHARLOTTE: It's your company.

CHARLES: Yes, but I don't make unilateral decisions. Profits
               drive everything.

CHARLOTTE: So racism is just an outgrowth of capitalism?
               Whites don't really believe they are better than
               the rest of us?

CHARLES: In the boardroom decisions are always color-
               blind. We don't get distracted. If this adminis-
               tration's base is solidly white men spewing racist
               rhetoric, it's not us.

ALEX: And white women . . . fifty-three percent . . .

CHARLOTTE: So in the boardroom, whites promoting and sup-
               porting themselves economically isn't racism and
               building private prisons is helping whom?

CHARLES: Have you any idea how many nonprofits I fund?

ALEX: Private prisons, nonprofits . . .

ERIC: Give it a rest, Alex.

ALEX: Mom's probably back in the kitchen crying again.

ERIC: I'll go see how Virginia's doing.

CHARLES: She'll be fine. I was just going to give her a hand.
                 (*He leaves.*)

CHARLOTTE: Eric, maybe this is not the best evening for us to—

ERIC: The best evenings are the evenings we have.
                 Look, if you are thrown by this prison thing—

CHARLOTTE: Thrown? Yes, but not surprised by the hypocrisy.
                 I understand that wealth touches every aspect of
                 life. I know how the system works. I have an in-
                 vestment portfolio, a retirement fund. It's just that
                 I thought Charles was making certain choices.

ERIC: Charles is a good man, he is highly respected
                 by everyone who works with him. He just told
                 me he's anxious to talk to you about a much big-
                 ger role at the foundation. This is a real oppor-
                 tunity for you. Do you realize the resources and
                 access you could have to do whatever work you
                 want? This is a perfect fit. So, over dessert let's
                 listen to what he has to say. I'm going to go give
                 them a hand so we can get this evening back
                 on track.

(Eric joins Virginia and Charles in the kitchen. Alex and Charlotte are left alone.)

ALEX: I just read an article called "White Fragility" by Robin DiAngelo . . . I should pass it on to my mother . . . though there is no end to her white tears.

CHARLOTTE: Aren't you being a bit hard on her?

ALEX: Tears can be very effective weapons. She's always using hers. I'm tired of it.

CHARLOTTE: She seems upset about your brother.

ALEX: My brother is upsetting.

CHARLOTTE: You seem upset. Are you angry?

ALEX: Angry? Yes, I'm angry at my father for incarcerating your people. Why aren't you?

CHARLOTTE: Why not just say people?

ALEX: Why not just answer my question?

CHARLOTTE: Isn't life more complicated than your question? Maybe you are angry at him for not doing everything he could to keep your brother out of prison?

ALEX: It seems pretty simple to me. You want your work supported by the very people you are critiquing.

CHARLOTTE: I could say the same of you.

ALEX: You could, but it's less of a choice for me . . .

CHARLOTTE: In any case, I'm not critiquing your family. I was invited to dinner.

ALEX: A dinner which is usually served by a black woman who was given the evening off. Wake up, Charlotte. He builds prisons.

CHARLOTTE: And hospitals and schools . . .

ALEX: And prisons.

CHARLOTTE: Maybe you should go check on your mother . . .

ALEX: Before you get in bed with my dad, understand he is willing to turn his back on his own son. Tim would be free if he wasn't a contradiction to the principles of my father's foundation.

CHARLOTTE: Can I ask what happened?

ALEX: He was a commodities trader with a heroin addiction. Now he's a nonreturning citizen for a year.

CHARLOTTE: Difficult to believe someone from your family couldn't work that out.

ALEX: My father watched my brother be handcuffed and dragged off to jail, and he did nothing to stop it. My dad is so sure about what he thinks he knows. Tim is a good guy, but living up to my dad's expectations is too much for anyone. I tried to help him. I'm sorry, I don't think we should give up on people.

CHARLOTTE: Maybe he didn't know what else to do, but that sounds difficult all around.

ALEX: I miss him. You wouldn't get it.

(*Eric, Charles, and Virginia reenter the room. Virginia carries dessert.*)

VIRGINIA: Dessert is served. Hazelnut cake with whipped cream and strawberries and fruit salad for the virtuous among us.

CHARLES: And I have ice wine from Canada.

ERIC: It's a dessert wine produced from grapes that have been frozen on the vine. Very rare. Charles is pulling out all the stops for you, Charlotte.

CHARLES: I think you'll find it delicious.

ALEX: Mom, are you okay?

VIRGINIA: Yes, I'm fine. Thank you, dear.

CHARLES: Charlotte, I may look conservative, but don't be fooled. The last year has showed us all that there is entrenched racism and xenophobia that no laws seem to alter. But the political moment can't be all that matters. Virginia and I have spent a lifetime

believing our intentions are good. We have
worked to be good people. The problem is our
country lacks moral imagination. This is where
you come in. Artists, like you, work from a different positioning. You can imagine beyond what is.

ERIC: Charlotte, you'll see that you and Charles have a
              shared vision about the role of art.

CHARLES: We need art to catapult us out of here. I'm
              investing in individuals who depict what is really
              happening out there in the daylight. Change can't
              precede recognition. I've been thinking about
              this a long time.

ALEX: There's a big gap between recognition and actual
              change. Throwing money at the wall is not the
              same as taking to the streets . . .

CHARLES: But, Alex, you've been out "on the street" as you
              say, and your protests have changed nothing.

ALEX: And your foundation—

CHARLES: (cuts off Alex) My foundation is one pathway
              to a new reality. I want you to be a part of this,
              Charlotte.

CHARLOTTE: Your desire for change is inspiring.

ERIC: Charles *is* offering you the ability to use your
              work to challenge how the public sees, instead
              of warehousing it like other collectors.

CHARLOTTE: I'm moved by your ambition to keep the work in the public eye.

ALEX: But isn't Dad simply using her work to stage his own "big picture"?

CHARLES: What the hell, Alex? Charlotte, if I collect your dead, they'll never be buried. You can be certain of that.

CHARLOTTE: My dead? Tell me, how is that about my work?

CHARLES: This entire evening, my dear, is about your work.

VIRGINIA: Charles, perhaps she'll understand if we show the piece we were so moved by. Shall we? Eric, will you help me?

CHARLES: Alex? (*Charles motions for Alex to help.*)

VIRGINIA: Charles purchased this sculpture for Alex, but you'll see it's in conversation with your work too. It's meant to be shown on the floor.

CHARLES: Alex, come give me a hand.

VIRGINIA: This is for you: *An Anatomy of a Death.*

(*Virginia pulls off the cloth.*)

(*Silence from everyone.*)

ALEX: Is that an autopsy report?

VIRGINIA: It's Michael Brown's autopsy report!

CHARLOTTE: (*to herself*) Michael Brown?

ALEX: (*quietly*) I can't even . . . You can't own Michael
                 Brown.

CHARLES: Wait. It's not Michael Brown.

ALEX: It's not? A minute ago you said you were collect-
                 ing Charlotte's dead. "They'll never be buried."
                 Remember?

CHARLES: I meant it metaphorically. This is a representation
                 of the violence against Brown.

CHARLOTTE: What do you mean it isn't Michael Brown?

CHARLES: Well, it's a photograph of a diagram. That dia-
                 gram documents the violence inflicted on a black
                 man. Isn't this the purpose of art—your art—
                 to make the invisible visible?

CHARLOTTE: Michael Brown's body was on the street for
                 hours. Isn't everything that happened to him
                 visible? This (*gestures toward the piece*) is not
                 revealing anything we haven't seen.

CHARLES: For me, to see exactly where and how many
                 bullets entered the body of this man, who is only
                 a year younger than Alex . . . was, to say the least,
                 upsetting.

VIRGINIA: I have to tell you, I felt sick. The entire incident was so violent and so unnecessary.

CHARLOTTE: It made you sick. It made you sad. And you bought *this*?

VIRGINIA: It affected us far more than all the accounts on television.

CHARLES: This autopsy is only about one thing. It gestures toward structural racism.

CHARLOTTE: And what does that mean?

CHARLES: It means the Ferguson police department was systemically harassing and arresting black citizens in Brown's neighborhood for years. This piece points to Officer Wilson. If it's a portrait of anyone, it's a portrait of him.

ALEX: It's Brown's autopsy.

CHARLOTTE: But according to you, Charles, the only way to get to Officer Wilson is through Michael Brown's body?

CHARLES: That body is a portal to the inhumanity.

CHARLOTTE: (*under her breath*) We're not going to get anywhere with this kind of . . . this kind of American sentimentality.

CHARLES: How is this sentimentality? This piece will remind everyone who comes into this house what's
happening out there.

CHARLOTTE: Feeling bad by looking at black lines enclosing
a white space doesn't come close to experiencing
the dread of knowing you could be killed for
simply being black.

ERIC: Not to state the obvious, but we're not black.
And I think that is what is important about your
work. It gives the viewer a point of entry.

CHARLOTTE: But we're not looking at my work. This generic
public record is just that, generic, impersonal.
Don't you understand people were shot in Bible
study? Nine bodies bleeding to death on a tile
floor is the same as this?

ERIC: Hold on, Charlotte. You are acting as if this is a
personal assault on you. It's not as if you run the
risk of being shot by police . . .

CHARLOTTE: If you think I am protected from ending up
like the Sandra Blands of the world—the black
woman who purportedly hanged herself . . .

VIRGINIA: We know who Sandra Bland is . . .

ERIC: I would have thought this piece is exactly the in-
tent of your work, to make people feel with their
eyes the violence done to African Americans.

CHARLES: I agree with Eric, this representation is no different from your work.

CHARLOTTE: Any police report of my death would erase me as much as this autopsy report erases Michael Brown.

CHARLES: I can't see this (*gestures toward the sculpture*) without thinking of Michael Brown. It's a memorial to him in our home.

ALEX: It's art in our house.

CHARLES: I know you're always saying the other pieces I collect aestheticize black experience, but you can't say that about this.

CHARLOTTE: If you think what I'm doing is no different than this then I fail.

VIRGINIA: But Charlotte, we want to buy your work too. We don't have to choose between autopsies and black art.

ALEX: You people are more than clueless.

CHARLOTTE: Oh my god.

ALEX: This just exposes your internalized racism. It's how you perform your white supremacy.

CHARLOTTE: Is this what I'm doing? Is this who I am?

ALEX: This is upper-class terrorism.

ERIC: This isn't one of your protests, Alex. You should check your privilege.

VIRGINIA: Why can't we all just get along?

ALEX: It doesn't matter what you say or what you do, you are just as blind and corrupted as every other white person. I can't believe you thought I would like this?

VIRGINIA: Aren't you always talking about the gated bubble we live in?

CHARLES: How can we get any closer to Brown's reality than this?

ALEX: You can get closer to actual living people, but you wouldn't know anything about that.

CHARLES: If only you knew how hard we tried with your brother.

ALEX: You belong in one of your prisons. Why don't you stay there for a year and then see if you'd buy this.

VIRGINIA: Alex, you're just being childish now.

ERIC: This is what comes from all the time he spends with his one-dimensional, sophomoric activist friends.

ALEX: You don't know a fucking thing about me.

CHARLES: I am waiting for the day you grow up!

ALEX: Fuck you, Dad!

(*Charlotte lies down in front of the autopsy piece, filling in for the missing body.*)

VIRGINIA: What's the matter with you, Alex?!

ERIC: This is the problem of mixing business with Alex's insufferable politics.

VIRGINIA: Fine, you hate it, but we bought it because we care, about you, about your brother, about Michael Brown.

ALEX: So *now* you care about Tim?

CHARLES: Don't use that tone with your mother. This is your doing, Ginny. First Tim and now look at Alex, no respect for what we've done, for who we are. My whole life has been about making the world better.

VIRGINIA: Better for black people maybe.

ALEX/CHARLES: Mom!/Ginny!

ERIC: Charlotte?

VIRGINIA: (*smoothing her clothes*) All this political injustice is important but not more important than your family.

CHARLES: Charlotte?

VIRGINIA: (*speaking to no one*) I don't know what we could have done better. We've failed . . . Did we fail? We failed something . . . (*Beat; she notices Charlotte.*) Charlotte?

(*Virginia, Alex, Eric, and Charles all look at Charlotte lying on the floor. Coltrane's "My Favorite Things" plays. Lights shift.*)

Scene Two

IMAGE ON REVERSE

Gilles Peress, *AFRICA. Rwanda. Kabgayi. April, 1994. Massacre site. Looters captured and killed at the Parish of Rukara church by government troops.*

IMAGE ON REVERSE

Jeff Wall, *Mimic*

IMAGE ON REVERSE
Kerry James Marshall, *Heirlooms and Accessories*

One year later. Charlotte is working in her studio. There is a knock on the door.

CHARLOTTE: Charles Spencer.

CHARLES: It's been awhile.

CHARLOTTE: Almost a year.

CHARLES: I appreciate you taking the time to see me at such short notice.

CHARLOTTE: I was happy to get your email this morning. I'm glad it worked out. How are Virginia and Alex?

CHARLES: They are both fine. We are all fine.

CHARLOTTE: Is Alex still doing his activism?

CHARLES: Still out on the streets. You should know, he mentioned you not long ago. He got it in his head that we should have apologized for not inviting other people of color to our dinner.

CHARLOTTE: Excuse me?

CHARLES: It was just that he felt we put you in the situation of explaining blackness . . . of speaking for all people of color.

CHARLOTTE: (*laughing*) Inviting more black people to explain would have spread out the work?

CHARLES: (*smiling*) I see your point.

CHARLOTTE: Alex is sweet, considerate too. In any case, Virginia did send me an apology. She said it wasn't your usual practice to devolve into a shouting arena at the end of dinner. That was kind of her.

CHARLES: Oh, I hadn't realized she'd been in touch.

CHARLOTTE: Did she TiVo the Australian Open again this year?

CHARLES: No, Serena wasn't playing. We watched Federer win his twentieth Grand Slam in real time. That was pretty exciting . . . tarnished, unfortunately, by that American from Tennessee who made the quarterfinals . . .

CHARLOTTE: With his Facebook page of white supremacy likes . . .

CHARLES: You know, it was a real disappointment to us that you decided to give the Charleston pieces to the Studio Museum.

CHARLOTTE: May I take your coat and scarf?

(*She folds them over a chair.*)

CHARLES: Do you have a darkroom?

CHARLOTTE: The last time I used one I was in school.

CHARLES: Really?

CHARLOTTE: I've always worked digitally. There is so much
               more freedom if you are willing to lose the
               romance of the darkness.

CHARLES: Touché. I see you're a Nikon person.

CHARLOTTE: My mother gave me that one for high school
               graduation.

CHARLES: Is this her? She's a beauty. I'm assuming that's
               your dad next to her.

CHARLOTTE: That's right.

CHARLES: Are you their only child?

CHARLOTTE: Yes, they were focused on their careers.

CHARLES: Ah. What do they do?

CHARLOTTE: Lawyer, doctor, except my father doesn't have
               patients. He tracks the path of diseases.

CHARLES: I thought you didn't shoot film.

CHARLOTTE: I don't. It was a gift to myself. I just think
               the cameras with their collapsible lenses are
               beautiful . . . It's what *I* collect.

CHARLES: You have others?

CHARLOTTE: It's a collection of one. It's from Berlin, 1936.

CHARLES: You know Ernst Leitz, who manufactured the Leica, helped get Jews out of Nazi Germany?

CHARLOTTE: Yes. The Leica Freedom Train.

CHARLES: Postwar, the Allies blew up photos of the emancipated Jews and the dead bodies in the camps and forced the Germans to look at them to combat anti-Semitism.

CHARLOTTE: Did it ever occur to you it could have the opposite effect? All those bodies could have fed their anti-Semitism.

CHARLES: You would have to be an animal to see it that way.

CHARLOTTE: Not an animal.

CHARLES: Whose photo is this? These corpses with the cloth covering them . . .

CHARLOTTE: It's taken by Gilles Peress.

CHARLES: Gilles Peress? Is he a person of color?

CHARLOTTE: What! He's white. He's a French Magnum photographer. Does documentary . . . Bosnia . . . Rwanda. (*Pause.*) Charles, why are you here? Are you shopping for more black death?

CHARLES:	You know where I went yesterday?
CHARLOTTE:	How would I know that?
CHARLES:	Eric took me to see your new show. That work was unrecognizable to me. What are you up to?
CHARLOTTE:	Up to? I take it you don't like it?
CHARLES:	What is there to like?
CHARLOTTE:	Wow. Fortunately, the critics don't share your opinion. Personally, I feel it's my most relevant work to date.
CHARLES:	Relevant to what? I have no idea what to feel about it.
CHARLOTTE:	That surprises me after everything that has happened in the past year. Charlottesville, DACA, "me too," our daily tweets, the indictments, the tax plan, "shithole countries," the government shutdown, the shooting in Las Vegas and the high school shooting in Parkland. What else?
CHARLES:	It has been a year, hasn't it. That's how the show felt to me, like a reaction. I have to admit, I wondered if it was a response to our dinner.
CHARLOTTE:	No . . . well . . . actually, yes—
CHARLES:	(*interrupts*) So it was the autopsy piece?

CHARLOTTE: But not because you bought it. I couldn't get what you said out of my head.

CHARLES: I said a lot of things. What exactly?

CHARLOTTE: That my work was no different from that piece. Not long after our dinner, I went to the Whitney Biennial. I was standing in front of the Emmett Till painting, the one that caused all the controversy, and all I could think about was your foundation. I kept wondering about your desire to collect black death. (*Speaking very slowly.*) I had this image of my work being held as in the hold of a ship. All that art just packed in like the dead and dying bodies themselves.

(*Beat.*)

CHARLES: Okay.

CHARLOTTE: I don't mean to suggest you shouldn't celebrate the work of black artists. It's the emphasis on black death that I needed to question for myself. What does it mean to portray black suffering as art? Just looking at the Charleston crime scene I realized what I wasn't seeing . . .

CHARLES: What weren't you seeing?

CHARLOTTE: You. Isn't that funny? I realized I wasn't seeing you.

CHARLES: But I'm not someone to look at . . .

CHARLOTTE: Aren't you? I can't stop thinking about those Michael Brown videos. It's like nobody could see the white officer because a black man died.

CHARLES: I know how much a part of this system I am, but I am not the officer with the gun.

CHARLOTTE: But you're locked into your imagination of black-ness just like that officer was locked into his . . . I really believe he thought he was being attacked. He certainly wasn't seeing the person in front of him. My god, how many bullet holes were in that autopsy piece of yours?

CHARLES: It was horrific, but my imagination of blackness and his are completely different. All white men don't look alike.

CHARLOTTE: (*she's been watching him*) Look, I don't want to think of the officer as a monster or Hulk Hogan or a demon or whatever and I don't think you're a monster, but his obsession with black people as criminals and yours with black people as victims are cut from the same cloth. Neither is human.

CHARLES: I just reject that. I am not someone controlled by an imagination I don't understand.

CHARLOTTE: Charles, we were all raised wrong. Art is not going to change laws, but it might make apparent something we didn't see about how we all grew up. At least that's what I hope for my own work.

CHARLES:	That's what my foundation's invested in. That's the point exactly.
CHARLOTTE:	You keep wanting to focus on black victims and dead black bodies. I understand that. But maybe we've been looking in the wrong direction. Walk it backwards. For example, look at this.
CHARLES:	Who are these women? Soccer moms?
CHARLOTTE:	Take a closer look.
CHARLES:	They seem to be mostly white women.
CHARLOTTE:	That's true. What else do you see?
CHARLES:	Is it a church group? There's an American flag. Maybe a town hall meeting for . . . for mothers, I don't know. Just tell me.
CHARLOTTE:	They're women in prison. The prison you built in Ohio. I doubt you would have said soccer moms if they were black.
CHARLES:	You don't know what I would have said because I don't know what I would have said!
CHARLOTTE:	In any case, your imagination, like mine, like everyone's, is a racial imagination, except you don't really think of yourself as having a race and being shaped by the beliefs of that race.

CHARLES:	My attention to black suffering is my attempt to get my whiteness out of your . . . our way.
CHARLOTTE:	Or your attention to black suffering allows you not to look at your own whiteness.
CHARLES:	I understand my relationship to privilege and power.
CHARLOTTE:	Well, all your attention to your whiteness didn't allow you to see the approaching white nationalists now in the White House.
CHARLES:	Many of us were shocked by what happened and is happening—
CHARLOTTE:	Some weren't and still aren't. This administration didn't beam down into our democracy. It's an amplification of what's always been here.
CHARLES:	We were focused on the bodies littering the streets and filling the prisons.
CHARLOTTE:	Your prisons . . .
CHARLES:	And shouldn't we have been? People were dying. Aggie Gund just sold a Lichtenstein for a hundred and fifty million to finance a criminal justice fund.
CHARLOTTE:	That's great, but black people have always been dying. And it's not because of "black-on-black

crime." Whites have only just noticed they themselves are doing the killing.

CHARLES: Here we are again! I truly am trying to find a way through.

CHARLOTTE: Charles, have you ever had the feeling you were all wrong?

CHARLES: All wrong?

CHARLOTTE: Completely misguided. I mean, I was making my work, but I didn't understand what the desire for it was all about. There I was, handing over black death spectacle.

CHARLES: "Black death spectacle"? That is just millennial rhetoric. That painting of Emmett Till only caused all that controversy because the artist was white. But I was moved by that painting, as I was moved by the painting of Philando Castile's murdered body at that same Whitney exhibition. No one objected to that painting, presumably because the painter was black.

CHARLOTTE: No, nobody objected to that painting because the artist has a developed craft and a deep consciousness of his history. If you recall, in the Philando Castile painting, the policeman with the gun is also present.

CHARLES: But what *moved* me was that both artists were reflecting back the victim.

CHARLOTTE: Maybe you think those artists are making those paintings for you, Charles, because the black body is in a state you're comfortable with.

CHARLES: I have news for you, they *are* making that work for me. Who the hell else is going to buy it? Not you. Do you really believe that dead and dying bodies are acceptable to me?

CHARLOTTE: Michael Brown, Freddie Gray, Eric Garner, Sandra Bland, Trayvon Martin, Philando Castile . . .

CHARLES: Okay.

CHARLOTTE: And any convictions?

CHARLES: But that doesn't turn me into a . . . a . . . a . . . can I get a glass of water?

(*Beat.*)

CHARLES: How old are you? How old were you in . . . in 1998?

CHARLOTTE: '98? In my early twenties. Why?

CHARLES: So, around the age Alex is now. Ginny and I had two toddlers then. On the news came the report that white supremacists dragged a black man to his death in Texas. A lynching by car. They tied him to the bumper and dragged him until his head and various other limbs detached from the trunk of his body. I had nightmares for months.

CHARLOTTE: I was about to graduate college. My mother
              called me. I remember not being able to get out
              of bed that day.

CHARLES: I thought all that was over. I remember being
              relieved the boys were young . . . because how to
              explain . . . I wanted them to inhabit . . . inherit
              a different world. I started doing what I could
              for . . . for . . .

CHARLOTTE: For me?

CHARLES: Fair enough, but also for me and for them, for
              the boys. The only thing I could think to do was
              find a way to prevent the forgetting. I don't want
              to contribute to the silence. Our silences. By
              showing work that exposes racism, I think I can
              keep our history in the forefront. Black deaths
              are a part of that history.

CHARLOTTE: But blackness can't be reduced to suffering if
              that means you lose the context and the history
              of how we got here. Let me show you something
              I've been thinking about. You must know the
              artist Kerry James Marshall?

CHARLES: I was at that Met Breuer opening, yes. It was
              crowded. Room after room of huge colorful
              paintings of black life.

CHARLOTTE: Did you notice this piece he calls *Heirlooms and
              Accessories*? It isolates the faces of white women
              watching a lynching and puts them in lockets.

CHARLES: I don't remember seeing this.

CHARLOTTE: I'm not surprised you didn't notice it. When Marshall turns his attention to black suffering, he sees the ordinary complicity of white people.

CHARLES: Are you saying the faces of the white women are more horrible than the images of the lynched men?

CHARLOTTE: In some ways, yes. That's only hard to accept because whiteness has been reduced to goodness in all of our psyches. I believed Dylann Roof's crime scenes should have been made public . . . And now I still think that . . . but the closer I got to those dead bodies the more inhumane I became. I was making objects of people to give to you. This realization upended my whole practice. I want you to consider these without you taking them personally. Treat it as research, as a form of study.

CHARLES: (*confusion in his voice*) That's me at Pace Gallery, that's me outside the Met Gala, Virginia and I at Lincoln Center . . . What is this? How did you . . .

CHARLOTTE: I went to openings and photographed you as I would any subject.

CHARLES: You what?

CHARLOTTE: A couple of months after our dinner, I was at the Lynette Yiadom-Boakye opening at the New

Museum and when I saw you I approached to say hello, but you didn't recognize me. In that moment, I felt like the artwork you collected. I was like an object you could be interested in or not depending on the day . . .

CHARLES: I didn't notice you in a crowd and you decided to stalk me?

CHARLOTTE: I photographed you at the event and you looked straight at the camera. See. This one here . . . After I printed this I thought I might do a series.

CHARLES: You had no right! I could sue you for invasion of privacy!

CHARLOTTE: These are public events . . .

CHARLES: (*speaking very slowly*) So your show that's getting all the great reviews . . . all those images of white skin wallpapering the gallery . . . I knew it, I knew it . . . Charlotte, is that my skin? Is that why it is called *Exhibit C*? Do I understand this correctly?

CHARLOTTE: Who cares whose skin it is? What difference does it make?

CHARLES: I care. *Exhibit C* cares. Do you think I'm an idiot?! This is fucking insane! I've worked so hard. I'd think you'd be grateful.

CHARLOTTE: Gratitude? Is that what you need from me?

CHARLES: I took an interest in you.

CHARLOTTE: Now I'm taking an interest in you. Come on.
Jesus, Charles, what's so wrong about talking
about whiteness? And who knows more about
being white than you?

CHARLES: (*very angry*) You know nothing about me. You
don't know how I've lived my life. You have no
idea what's in my heart. (*Charles grabs her by the
shoulders.*) What is it you think you know?!

CHARLOTTE: What are you doing?

CHARLES: (*releasing Charlotte*) Charlotte, look at me. Tell
me what *you* see? Do you see anything beyond
our history?

CHARLOTTE: Charleston, Charlottesville, that's what I know.
Our history. The present. What do you mean
beyond? Beyond what?

CHARLES: Can you even see Charles Spencer? Tell me that
you understand I am not that history. Tell me
that you see me.

CHARLOTTE: All I've been doing is looking at you for months.
It's like you're Moses. Doors open for you. People
step aside for you. You have so much mobility.
Charles, what do you want me to say?

CHARLES: If I am only ever a white man to you, how far
will that get us?

CHARLOTTE: What do you see when you look at me?

CHARLES: The daylight.

CHARLOTTE: What does that even mean?

CHARLES: You of all people should understand that. You and I are out in the world and it's as if there's a fault line that runs the entirety of our lives between us. On your terms there's no way for me to get to you on the other side.

CHARLOTTE: If that were only true. Despite all the segregation, the tragedy is we are on the same side. We've always been here together, shipwrecked here together.

CHARLES: You're right; we're here together.

CHARLOTTE: Wrecked together, solitary, here together . . .

CHARLES: But the feeling is the feeling of a gap.

CHARLOTTE: The gap, Charles, is caused because you refuse the role you actually play.

CHARLES: I don't need you to show me me.

CHARLOTTE: Me, me, me. You don't need me to show you anything. That's probably the first honest thing you've said.

CHARLES: Fuck you, Charlotte.

CHARLOTTE: I'm already fucked. You know, I have to admit,
I thought you were different from all the others,
but in the end . . . for you I'm just this annoyance
that won't conform to your good works.

CHARLES: You're acting as if I think of you as some kind of
project.

CHARLOTTE: Well, don't you?

CHARLES: I do believe I can help.

CHARLOTTE: If you actually want to help, why don't you make
you your project?

CHARLES: What about me? My money? My power? My mobility, as you say?

CHARLOTTE: I mean the mass murder and devastation that
comes with you being you.

CHARLES: Me being me? Mass murder, devastation. It's hard
not to hear that as a completely irrational attack.

CHARLOTTE: Racism exists outside of reason. Black people
have never been human.

CHARLES: That is so hopeless.

CHARLOTTE: Go further into that hopelessness, and then we
can begin to really see each other.

CHARLES: You're right to keep me a part of it. My white-ness. It needs to be faced.

CHARLOTTE: (*she faces Charles*) At its deepest level, yes.

CHARLES: It's just skin and yet I know it's power too.

CHARLOTTE: Dehumanizing power.

CHARLES: What is skin? I've heard dust is mostly skin (*touching the table*)—is this my skin? Yours?

CHARLOTTE: Charles—

CHARLES: We're shedding skin all the time—thousands of cells a minute. But it renews itself. I've never actually looked at my skin.

How many cells is it? How porous is it? How many layers are there? Where is it darkest? Where lightest? (*He begins to unbutton his shirt.*) All my skin is holding me together. Good lord, all this skin shields me. It protects me from . . . from being you.

It's like the badge of the police. (*He removes his shirt and turns his back to her.*) I'm ready. (*Beat.*)

Charlotte, you can shoot me now. (*He stands there with his back to her and arms at his side. Silence.*)

(Leonard Cohen's "Different Sides" begins to play. Charlotte ties her smock around her waist and, taking off her shoes, steps onto a crate, binding her hands with his scarf. She stares at Charles's back. Charles turns around. His horror and confusion are apparent. There is the click and flash of a camera.)

THE END

ILLUSTRATION CREDITS

CLAUDIA RANKINE is the author of five books, including *Citizen: An American Lyric*, which was a *New York Times* best seller and winner of the National Book Critics Circle Award, the *Los Angeles Times* Book Prize, the Forward Prize, and many other awards. In 2016, Rankine co-founded the Racial Imaginary Institute (TRII). She is a MacArthur Fellow and the Frederick Iseman Professor of Poetry at Yale University.

claudiarankine.com

The text of *The White Card* is set in Adobe Garamond Pro.
Book design by Rachel Holscher.
Composition by Bookmobile Design and Digital
Publisher Services, Minneapolis, Minnesota.
Manufactured by Versa Press on acid-free,
30 percent postconsumer wastepaper.